Clean
THIS!

Clean
THIS!

320 Reasons to Stop Cleaning

By Mary McHugh

Illustrations by Adrienne Hartman

**Andrews McMeel
Publishing**

Kansas City

06 07 08 09 10 BID 10 9 8 7 6 5 4 3 2 1

ISBN-13: 978-0-7407-5720-4
ISBN-10: 0-7407-5720-2

Library of Congress Control Number: 2005932779

Illustrations copyright © 2006 by Adrienne Hartman
Book design by Holly Camerlinck
Composition by Steve Brooker at Just Your Type

www.andrewsmcmeel.com

Attention: Schools and Businesses
Andrews McMeel books are available at quantity discounts with bulk purchase for
educational, business, or sales promotional use. For information, please write to:
Special Sales Department, Andrews McMeel Publishing, 4520 Main Street,
Kansas City, Missouri 64111.

Let's face it–nobody really likes to clean. There are a thousand things to do that are more fun and more important. But somehow we have to have a clean house, clean clothes, and clean children so the neighbors won't call the health inspector and our husbands won't leave us for a neater person.

I have come up with more than three hundred ingenious reasons to avoid cleaning, things to do instead of cleaning, and when all else fails, ways to get the cleaning done (or at least give the illusion that you have cleaned) with the least amount of effort from you–things like inviting all the neighborhood kids over for a dog-washing/pizza party when your dog is really smelly. (Just don't let any of the kids in your home afterward.) Spray lemon-scented furniture polish into the air in your living room and people will assume you've dusted. Persuade a TV producer to do a reality show in your house—then his crew will have to clean it. If your husband needs cleaning, ask those five gay guys to come over and neaten him up.

There are all kinds of ways to get the rotten jobs done without your actually moving a muscle. And with all that time you spend not cleaning, you can learn to play the harp, take your child to the circus, sail over the countryside in a hot-air balloon, or take your mother to lunch. Remember: If God had meant us to clean all the time, he wouldn't have given us a brain.

1.

Did you ever try to have a conversation with someone who loves to clean?

2.

My favorite person is a woman I once met who declared when she got married that she would never do laundry–and has sent it out ever since.

3.

Don't disturb the cobwebs.
They make wonderful
Halloween decorations.

4.

Lots of children love to vacuum.
Exploit this fact.

5.

With any luck, your mother-in-law's
eyesight will get weaker as she gets
older, and she'll think you've become
a terrific housekeeper.

6.

There are no Pulitzer Prizes
for Best Housekeeper.

7.

Tell visitors, "I don't care if you write your initials in the dust on my table–just don't date it."

8.

Follow Roseanne's example:
"I'm not going to vacuum until
Sears makes one you can ride on."

9.

It'll just be dirty again on Thursday.

10.

You could be learning to
play the clarinet.

11.

Twenty-five years from now, who will care if your house was spotless all the time?

12.

People come to see **you**,
not your waxed floors.

13.

You have a choice: Clean out
your closets or meet a friend
for lunch. It's a no-brainer.

14.

I've never understood
people who say,
"When I'm stressed,
I scrub the kitchen floor."

15.

"Cleanliness is next to godliness" refers to your personal hygiene, not your house.

16.

If you can't see through your windows, buy some really pretty curtains.

17.

Just as you're about to clean out the refrigerator, your husband wants to make love. The refrigerator will still be there tomorrow.
Will your husband?

18.

Your two-year-old wants
to go to the park—now.

19.

Plant a lilac bush.

20.

Buy carpets the same color as the mud your children track into the house.

21.

If you can't stand the sight of a speck of dust in your house, get out of the house and go to a movie.

22.

Nowhere in the marriage ceremony does it say, "I promise to clean the house every day."

23.

Put gray countertops in the kitchen—they hide a multitude of sins.

24.

You've got dust bunnies as
big as small dogs under the bed?
If anyone looks under the bed,
tell them they **are** small dogs.

25.

Your teenagers need money to buy CDs. Your house needs cleaning. See the connection?

26.

When your children leave home to go to college or to get married, you'll never need to clean again if you've trained your husband properly.

27.

Leave the dishes in the sink and go for a bike ride in the springtime.

28.

One of the most beloved characters in comic strips is Pigpen in **Peanuts**.

29.

What's more important? A clean kitchen floor or a child who wants to be read to?

30.

When you're ninety, do you want to look back on clean bathrooms as your major accomplishment?

31.

Do you want the only thing they can think of to say at your funeral to be "Her house was really clean"?

32.

If your children refuse to clean their rooms, forget it. **They'll** have to find a place for their friends to sit down.

33.

Will your children remember
the living room as a place they
weren't allowed to play in?

34.

Would you rather have your grown
children say, "The house was always
clean," or "My mother was always
there to do things with us"?

35.

If you just **have** to clean, make strawberry shortcake with lots of whipped cream, and clean up after that.

36.

You just started to clean the oven and your best friend needs to talk to you about her husband's rotten ex-wife. The oven will still be there later.

37.

Your three-year-old has made a huge mess painting a picture of you. Give her a big hug, take her out for an ice cream cone, and worry about the mess later.

38.

Your grandchildren have
come to visit and there's chaos
everywhere. Enjoy it!

39.

Get rid of your kitchen.
All you really need are
some vending machines
and a large trash can.

40.

The only reason to clean is to put off doing something else.

41.

Put forty-watt bulbs in all
your lamps and no one will
see the dust.

42.

Silverware has a nicer sheen if
you don't polish it so much.

43.

Real friends don't see the mess in your house because their houses look the same.

44.

A clean desk is a sign of
a sterile mind.

45.

A cluttered desk makes you
look busy and important.

46.

When you run out of clean underwear, go to Victoria's Secret and buy some more.

47.

Linen napkins are unsanitary.

48.

Didn't you ever hear the saying "Everyone eats a peck of dirt in his lifetime"?

49.

Sweep more than your troubles under the rug.

50.

Have your bridal registry at Hallmark
and ask for beautiful paper plates,
cups, napkins, and tablecloths.

51.

There's the oil-polish school and
the wax-polish school. For you,
school is out.

52.

Let the coasters stick to the tables. Then you'll know where they are when you need them.

53.

Water rings on the coffee table
just show how many great
parties you've had.

54.

Sleep in the nude and you won't
have to wash pajamas.

55.

Waxed floors are dangerous.
Someone might slip and sue you.

56.

Don't even consider buying a house
without a self-cleaning oven.

57.

Use your stove for storage instead of cooking, and you'll never have to clean it.

58.

If you must cook,
don't fry anything because
of all that spattered grease
you'll have to clean up.
Just boil everything.

59.

Brooms are for witches.

60.

It's expensive to have that waxy buildup on your kitchen floor removed, so don't wax them in the first place.

61.

Would you rather be Felix or Oscar from **The Odd Couple**?

62.

Evolution: Grandma used a washboard. Mother used a washing machine. You send it out.

63.

Lots of cleaning leads to red, rough hands.

64.

Forget crystal chandeliers and all that Windex. Get track lighting.

65.

Teflon is a woman's best friend.

66.

Disposable paper cups
don't use up any room
on your shelves.

67.

You could be riding a motorcycle down Main Street.

68.

A full ashtray discourages smoking.

69.

You could be riding the
Ferris wheel in Paris.

70.
___

Dirty screens keep out more flies.

71.
___

**You can't have children without dirt.
It's a fact of life.**

72.

Moldy shower stalls discourage houseguests.

73.

A cluttered attic is a sign
of a rich life.

74.

A cluttered attic shows you've
had a colorful past.

75.

A cluttered attic means your children have left home—finally!

76.

A messy child is a happy child.

77.

Keep your husband in a cage
with a removable floor.

78.

Leave your husband's dirty socks on the floor. Just paint over them.

79.

When every dish in the house is dirty, eat out.

80.

Don't cry over spilled milk. Buy a cat.

81.

A new broom sweeps clean.
No broom saves you a lot of work.

82.

Throw all those moldy leftovers in
your refrigerator into a casserole
and take it to the next church supper.

83.

SOS stands for Save Our Ship, but SOS pads never saved anyone.

84.

Who's kidding whom that Bon Ami is a good friend?

85.

Heloise has made a fortune with cleaning tips. You never will.

86.

Encourage your friends to sit on the couch covered with dog hairs—they can take them home with them and you won't have to vacuum the couch.

87.

Polish your floors by skating across them in your bunny slippers.

88.

Become an artist. No one will expect you to clean anything.

89.

Don't bother to clean out your cupboards—expiration dates don't mean anything.

90.

You could be having tea
with an old friend.

91.

You could be sailing
on a sunset cruise.

92.

If God meant us to clean, we'd have mops instead of feet.

93.

Nobody ever changed the world cleaning a bathroom.

94.

Dust is unsanitary.
Stay away from it!

95.

Cleaning agents can be hazardous to your health. Throw them all away.

96.

Cleaning robots are just around the corner. Wait for them.

97.

When your children are grown and gone, you'll have a permanently clean home without even trying. But it's not as much fun.

98.

If dirt bothers you, take off your glasses. Better still, make your guests take off their glasses at the door.

99.

A woman without a
house to clean is like
a fish without a bicycle.

100.

Your daughter-in-law will love you if
you step over the mess in her house
to play with your grandchildren.

101.

It takes a heap of messin' to
make a house a home.

102.

Remember: The dust will be
here long after you are. In fact,
you'll be dust someday.

103.

Don't disturb that dust
on your table. It might
be your grandfather.

104.

Squeaky clean is for mice.

105.

Stop thinking of paper plates as just for picnics.

106.

As Scarlett would say,
"Tomorrow is another day,"
so clean up the mess
tomorrow.

107.

You could be drinking champagne
in a hot-air balloon.

108.

The dust will win, you know.

109.

Why are you cleaning the house before the cleaning woman comes? Nobody is paying **you**.

110.

Slobs are born, not made.
Don't fight it.

111.

"Don't clean up the mess,"
Freud said. "I know exactly where
everything is." Case closed.

112.

Cleanliness is just another word for obsessive-compulsive behavior.

113.

Everybody hates a perfectionist.

114.

If your house is clean all the time, you're not having enough fun.

115.

To clean or not to clean?
Even Hamlet could
decide that one.

116.

You could be hang gliding.

117.

You could be sharing a
hot tub with Brad Pitt.

118.

Did you ever hear of
anyone becoming rich or
famous for cleaning?

119.

If you never cook, you never have to clean up. Two very good things.

120.

Why would **anyone** clean behind the refrigerator? What kind of a nut looks there?

121.

Whatever lurks behind your couch, let it lurk.

122.

You could be riding a camel
along the Nile.

123.

Paint beautiful trompe l'oeil
pictures on all your windows and
you'll never have to wash them.

124.

Don't clean under couch cushions—just look for money there and leave the dirt.

125.

Have only short friends—
then they won't be able to
see the dirt on top of things.

126.

You could be learning to tango.

127.

Paint a picture.

128.

Make everyone take off their shoes before they come into your house. Explain that you're part Japanese.

129.

Entertain by candlelight so no one will see the dirt. Keep telling your guests how great they look in dim light.

130.

Dogs leave muddy footprints
and poop everywhere.
Get a nice clean cat instead.

131.

Don't let your grown children
come back to live in your house.
They take a lot of cleaning up after.

132.

You could be dating
Prince William in London.

133.

If your drinking glasses have spots on them, tell your guests to connect the dots and give a prize for the best design.

134.

Put dishes directly into the dishwasher without rinsing first—that's its **job**.

135.

Do not think of marrying any man who cannot provide you with a self-cleaning oven, a self-defrosting refrigerator, and a dishwasher. If you do not wish to marry, provide these things for yourself instead of jewelry.

136.

Think of that film of dirt on
your windows as an SPF factor of
fifteen **protecting** you against
the aging rays of the sun.

137.

If your husband points out that the
light fixtures need dusting, say,
"What? And spoil the mood?"

138.

Pet hair on the couch and chairs makes wonderful stuffing for toys for underprivileged children.

139.

If company is coming, throw all your junk in one room and close the door. Tell your guests there's a fierce dog in there that bites.

140.

You could be kayaking.

141.

All you need is the illusion of cleaning: Mix some pine-scented cleaner with water in a spray bottle and mist the air lightly.

142.

Leave some wet rags around, collapse on the sofa, and say, "I clean and clean and I'll just have to do it again tomorrow."

143.

You could be skydiving.

144.

Throw some cinnamon in a pie pan in the oven and tell people you've been making cookies for the school bake sale and didn't have time to clean.

145.

Put some get-well cards on the mantle and tell people you've been too sick to clean.

146.

Hug your dog.

147.

Martha Stewart has a very clean house and look what happened to **her**!

148.

The morning after a big party, tiptoe out of the house and don't come back until evening. Maybe fairies and elves will come and clean it.

149.

Persuade some TV producer to do
a reality show in your house.
Then **they'll** have to clean it.

150.

If you must have an absolutely
clean, sterile, immaculate house,
move to an operating room.

151.

Make brownies.

152.

Spray lemon-scented furniture polish into the air in your living room and people will assume you've dusted.

153.

Move to Japan.
There's no furniture to
clean, no rugs to vacuum,
no beds to make, and only
a few rice bowls to wash.

154.

You could be flying a kite on Cape Cod.

155.

If you **must** clean (somebody reported you to the health inspector), make it fun: Dust when **Seinfeld** reruns are on; wear headphones and dance to Billy Joel while you're vacuuming; talk to your best friend while you're cleaning the kitchen counters.

156.

Give your husband a copy of **Clean Like a Man: Housekeeping for Men and the Women Who Love Them** by Tom McNulty and hope he tries out some of the ideas in there. At the very least he won't be stirring up any more mess to clean up while he's reading it.

157.

Tell people you don't clean because you're a hand model.

158.

Learn to play the piano.

159.

You can tell people who love to
clean floors by their lumpy knees.

160.

You know how people are always saying, "I don't do windows"? Well, make your motto, "I don't do windows or floors or toilets or sinks or rugs or kitchens or laundry."

161.

If you leave a film on your bathroom tile, you can write messages on it for your spouse, making sure he will remember to bring home some beer.

162.

You know those ads where a woman is lying in a hammock, smiling, reading a book, and she looks up and says, "I'm cleaning my oven"? Buy whatever she uses and spray it everywhere and stay in the hammock.

163.

If the urge to clean comes
over you (fat chance!),
leave the house immediately
and don't come back until
the urge is gone.

164.

Don't polish the furniture.
Buy a sheep dog for that.

165.

If you live alone and never
have guests, why would you ever
think of cleaning?

166.

Let Tennessee Williams characters
collect a dust-attracting glass
menagerie, not you.

167.

If you still have venetian blinds on
any of your windows, give them to
the next needy Venetian you meet
and stop cleaning all those slats.

168.

If your refrigerator coils
need dusting, persuade
your cat to run by them
several times. If he refuses
(and he probably will)
get the dog to do it.
Dogs will do anything
for a "Good dog!"

169.

Is your walk-in closet so full of stuff only Stuart Little could walk into it? Just seal it up and start a new closet.

170.

Is your TV screen so dusty you can barely make out Matt Lauer's face in the morning? Don't be a slob. Wipe it off with your nightgown.

171.

Sing to your cat.

172.

Make love to your husband.

173.

The only reason to clean out the drawers in the kitchen is if you haven't been able to find your car keys for three days and they miss you at work.

174.

You won't have to clean out the refrigerator in the summertime if you keep only the essentials in there: champagne, beer, and your underwear.

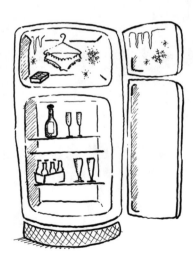

175.

If your house is such a mess you don't know where to start, don't start. Go to the beach.

176.

Don't **look** for things to clean. You'll find them.

177.

When you move into your new apartment, put the stove in storage, install a dishwasher in its place, and buy a microwave.

178.

Give your children their own individual little sponges and let them scrub the tiles while they're having their baths.

179.

If your husband is the cause of most of the mess in your house, make a list of his good points and weigh them against the mess. If he has more than five good points, learn to live with the mess. If he has fewer than five points . . .

180.

If your children's rooms are full of cookie crumbs and broken potato chips, give them DustBuster vacuums for their next birthdays. They'll hate you, but it will give them something to tell their psychiatrists later on.

181.

Meet a friend at Starbucks.

182.

Unless you plan to have dinner
parties in the garage, don't
waste your time cleaning it.
Cover the floor with a nice Audi.

183.

Invite all your friends over
for a Paint-the-Kitchen party
and tell them you've only
invited your A-list friends
for the privilege.

184.

The cleanest person I know has just been diagnosed with an obsessive-compulsive disorder. Don't let that happen to you.

185.

Play with your children.

186.

If you insist on cleaning your house yourself, you're putting a lot of hard-working cleaning women out of business.

187.

Before she died, my grandmother said if she had her life to live over she'd spend much less time cleaning and much more time making a mess.

188.

Get a new kitchen floor that looks like freshly ground pepper. Tell everyone it's the latest thing.

189.

When you go out to eat, always order food the same color as whatever you're wearing. Then the stains won't show.

190.

If the light beige upholstery in your car has stains from a spilled orange soda, connect the spots for a colorful work of art and tell people it was an extra when you bought the car.

191.

If your car trunk is full of needles from last year's Christmas tree, don't vacuum them out. It's almost next Christmas and another tree will be along any minute.

192.

A sparkling clean, brilliantly waxed
car is more likely to be stolen.

193.

Tell your teenager that state law
requires drivers with learner's
permits to wash the car once
a week in order to qualify for
a permanent license.

194.

Some wax products can scratch the finish on your car. Don't take a chance. Leave your car unwashed and unwaxed.

195.

When it comes to cleaning, make **mañana** your motto.

196.

Never clean out the glove compartment in your car. Something you've been looking for for years might be in there.

197.

Encourage your children to wear wet bathing suits in the car so they can wash the leather upholstery as they jump around and hit each other.

198.

Don't dust. Just attach a dust cloth to your dog's tail so he can clean off the furniture when he wags his tail. Keep saying, "Good dog," and he'll dust until his tail falls off.

199.

When you have a backyard barbecue, have guests draw numbers from a hat. The one with the lowest number gets to clean the grill. He may never come back, but you've got lots of other friends.

200.

When your new daughter-in-law comes to visit, ask her to show you all her favorite cleaning tricks. Keep asking her until the house is spotless.

201.

When your son-in-law comes over, ask him if he has any special tricks for washing the car. Ask him to show them to you.

202.

Grow flowers.

203.

Leave a bottle of tile cleaner in the guest bathroom with a note on it saying PLEASE USE ME.

204.

Don't flip your mattress. Just put the pillows at the other end and sleep by the footboard. It will give you a whole new perspective.

205.

If your father-in-law gets hair oil on one place on the headboard of the guest bed, ask him to lean against a different place each night, until the whole headboard is evenly oiled.

206.

When your dog is **really** dirty, invite all the neighborhood kids over for a dog-washing/pizza party. Don't let any of the kids in your home afterward.

207.

Consumer Reports says bronze has a much nicer patina when you don't polish it. Are you going to argue with **Consumer Reports?**

208.

Invite some kids over and give a prize for the best sculpture made of candlestick wax—they have to pick it off the candlesticks first, of course.

209.

A glass of wine in the late afternoon makes your whole house seem perfect—cleaned or uncleaned.

210.

Spots on your glassware?
Give your guests straight vodka
and the spots will blend in.

211.

Remember: Your house won't
smell of strong cooking odors
if you don't cook.

212.

If your patio furniture is covered with bird droppings, paint it white.

213.

Install a dimmer in the dining room so you'll never have to clean the 158 little pieces of glass in the chandelier.

214.

Do **not** clean your fireplace. Get one of those fancy Japanese fans to cover up the whole mess.

215.

Keep cutting boards spotless
by always ordering takeout.

216.

Look for household products with
the word "Microban" on them and
no matter how little you clean,
your house will be germ-free.

217.

For a really clean bathroom,
always shower at your health
club instead of at home.
And you'll be thinner, too!

218.

Coffee stains do not come out,
I don't care what Heloise says.
So switch to tea.

219.

Don't bother to clean
your computer. It will be obsolete
just after you clean it and you'll
have to buy a new one anyway.

220.

Your aluminum pots and pans will stay shiny and clean if you switch to a diet of fruits and raw vegetables. And you'll be so healthy!

221.

You'll never have to polish
those copper pots if you
just hang them on the
wall as decorations.

222.

Are your diamonds dirty?
Get a better job and buy new ones.

223.

If you're housebreaking your dog,
buy poop-colored rugs.

224.

Never finish any sentence in a household hints book that starts out, "Scrub a fishing rod handle with . . ."

225.

Don't worry about cleaning
up bloodstains—just get out
of the country.

226.

Never buy any item of
clothing that says
WASH BY HAND on the care label.

227.

Nobody under forty knows what "spring cleaning" means.

228.

There's no need to clean your deck—that's what rain is for.

229.

Don't use your grandmother's china if you can't put it in the dishwasher. Just display it somewhere.

230.

Barbie's entourage should include
a cleaning woman so your daughter
can learn what's important
when she's a mommy.

231.

Clean your glasses only once a
week–then you won't see the dirt.

232.

The reason your grandmother's house was always clean was because she had nothing else to do. **You** do.

233.

Marry a man whose mother was a feminist who believed a husband should do housework, laundry, and diaper changing.

234.

Buy an electric litter box that cleans up after your cat.
Your whole mood will change.

235.

When your husband's favorite chair for watching TV and drinking beer becomes really gross, throw a sheet over it, put ties around the legs, and say your decorator did it.

236.

When your husband's beard has crumbs in it, kiss them away.

237.

If your car has more junk in it than your basement, have a yard sale.

238.

When your wooden floors get dirty, just stain them a darker color.

239.

If your sink is full of dirty dishes, trade your teenager a ride to the mall for a dishwasher full of clean dishes.

240.

Buy a bigger clothes hamper and wash less often.

241.

When your children get
dirty, send them outside
to play so you don't have
to look at them.

242.

If your husband needs cleaning up,
call the five gay guys on TV to
neaten him up.

243.

If you notice stains on the front of your mother's dress, turn her sideways in her chair.

244.

Don't put food in the fridge and it won't rot. Buy everything in cans if you must eat in.

245.

Put the hamster cage in
the oven to remind you not
to cook and cause splatters.
If you forget, just buy
another hamster.

246.

If basements were meant to
be cleaned, they'd be called
"the main floor."

247.

I once met a woman who cleaned
her attic before a dinner party.
She's in an institution now.

248.

Don't clean your closets—
they were invented to
store a whole bunch of
stuff you never use.

249.

Buy tablecloths that come to the floor and nobody will see the crumbs under there.

250.

No child understands the words,
"Clean up your room," so just
close the door to his room
and don't go in there.

251.

Buy the only pet that doesn't
need washing—a sponge.

252.

If your grandfather is covered with crumbs, put him outside in the yard for the birds to clean up.

253.

Persuade your children to string all the popcorn under the couch cushions together for a Christmas tree decoration.

254.

If your rubies and sapphires are dirty, say to yourself, "Who's going to notice?"

255.

If your child comes home with a dirty face, pick her up and kiss her. In a few years that face will be clean all the time and she won't let you kiss her.

256.

Flour all over the counter means your family will love you a lot while they're eating that cherry pie.

257.

If your mother's dress from the thrift shop has a stain, just tell her it's part of the pattern so she won't worry.

258.

Has your sister with clinical depression stopped bathing? Run her through the car wash.

259.

Has your teenage son worn the same shirt five days in a row? Spray him with Febreze and he'll smell fine again.

260.

Do you have a friend who keeps giving you helpful cleaning tips? Ask her to demonstrate—several times a month.

261.

The Collier brothers were famous for their messy house. You could be famous too if you stopped straightening up and throwing things out.

262.

There's such a thing as **too** clean. Don't risk it.

263.

How many housewives does it take to clean a kitchen? None, if she has trained her family right.

264.

Maybe your mirror would be a little kinder to you if you stopped cleaning it.

265.

Tap-dance.

266.

Live in a hotel.

267.

Give each member of your family a
refrigerator magnet that shows
a washing machine and the words
DO YOUR OWN DAMN LAUNDRY.

268.

The world is waiting for the first female president of the United States. That could be you if you would **stop cleaning**.

269.

Why would you even **think** about cleaning when there's a service called "Merry Maids" who must just **love** cleaning?

270.

Open a new file in your PC called "Housework." Send it to the Recycle Bin. Empty the Recycle Bin. When your computer asks you, "Are you sure you want to delete "Housework" permanently?" Click on "Yes."

271.

Your house doesn't pass the white-glove test? Luckily no one wears white gloves anymore.

272.

You could be starring on Broadway as the slob in **The Odd Couple**.

273.

Marry a nearsighted man and hide his glasses.

274.

You could be swimming with dolphins.

275.

Whose bright idea was it that women get to do all the dirty jobs in the house anyway?

276.

If your ceilings are cobwebby, invite only short, nearsighted people over.

277.

You have to clean toddlers—there's no getting around it. The best part is wrapping them in a large towel and hugging them dry.

278.

Don't dust piano keys—let the cat run up and down on them. There's even a song about it called "Kitten on the Keys."

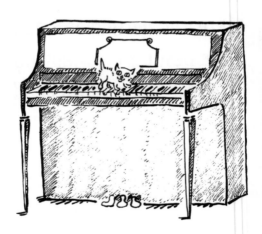

279.

Teddy bears are just naturally clean. I don't think Pooh ever took a bath.

280.

Encourage your teenager to start his own band and tell him he can practice in the garage if he cleans and paints it first.

281.

Shoot your golf balls into water traps as often as possible and they'll be sparkling clean.

282.

Give any books that haven't been read in so long they are dusty to the local library.

283.

Try to ignore your teenager's messy room when she wants to talk to you and just listen. The messy room will still be there when she goes to college, but she won't.

284.

If you can still tell whether it's raining or sunny when you look out your windows, they don't need washing yet.

285.

When your mother asks if she can do "a little cleaning, dear," when she comes to babysit, hug her and say, "I'd love it." Don't take it as an insult.

286.

How many men does it take to unload the dishwasher? None. No man has ever done it.

287.

Cover your bathroom floors with soft rugs and you'll never have to scrub the floors again.

288.

Persuade your husband to clean the whole house some day (say you're sick or something) and I guarantee you'll have a cleaning woman the next week.

289.

Is your living room floor covered with toys at the end of the day? Hire Mary Poppins to come and snap her fingers so all the toys will march into their boxes. Sing along with her.

290.

Watch **Roseanne** reruns and you'll notice she never cleans and her house looks fine—well, at least it's not filthy.

291.

Don't drink and clean—you might clean something twice by mistake.

292.

Pearl necklaces become
more lustrous the more
you wear them because
of the oils in your skin,
so don't ever clean them.

293.

Family photos in frames on tabletops are dust catchers. Put them in one giant frame and hang it on the wall.

294.

If you have a harp, don't clean it. Just play it all the time and it will stay clean. You'll have lots of friends, too.

295.

Take a long bubble bath every day
with scented candles and a good book
to read and you'll never have to clean
the bathtub. You'll also be the most
relaxed person in the neighborhood.

296.

Making chocolate fudge
brownies with chocolate
chips isn't really messy when
you have children to
lick the bowl clean.

297.

If you **must** clean something, get in the tub with your husband and scrub his back.

298.

People with **really** clean homes
cover their furniture with plastic.
Nobody ever visits them.

299.

If God meant for you to clean
all the time, he wouldn't have
given you a brain.

300.

Love means never
having to say,
"I can't go with
you—I'm cleaning."

301.

Think of rainy days as
wash-your-car days
and leave your car
in the driveway.

302.

When your three-year-old
has chocolate ice cream
all over her face, kiss it clean.

303.

When your fourteen-year-old
gives up bathing, send him out
for long walks in the rain.

304

Plant only short trees around your house so you won't have to clean the leaves from the gutters.

305.

Don't throw away all your old
scarves and costume jewelry.
What will your granddaughters
play dress-up in?

306.

Don't marry a man who
is allergic to dust.

307.

When your refrigerator needs cleaning, fill the house with teenagers, lock them in the kitchen, and don't let them out until the fridge is picked clean.

308.

You could be driving along a country road in Vermont after the leaves have changed to deep red, yellow, and orange.

309.

You will have hours and hours of non-laundry time when your last child goes off to college. Use it to learn to paint or sing or fly a plane.

310.

Show me a fanatic cleaner and
I'll introduce you to her
children's psychiatrist.

311.

Every house should have
a mudroom. It takes away a lot of
guilt. It's **supposed** to be dirty.

312.

Erma Bombeck said,
"If I had my life to live over,
I would sit on the grass with
my children and not worry
about grass stains." She also
said, "Housework, if you
do it right, will kill you."
Erma Bombeck was a very
wise woman.

313.

How many husbands does it
take to clean the average house?
None—they're all busy that day.

314.

If your house at the beach always
has sand on the floor, teach
everybody to do a soft shoe
dance and enjoy it.

315.

When was the last time you used all those silver trays and bowls you got as wedding gifts that you have to keep polishing? Give them to your daughter-in-law—the one who loves housework—and she'll think you're a fantastic mother-in-law.

316.

According to psychiatrist Theodore Shapiro, "Messiness is just the natural state of all children until age six." It's natural—let them be messy!

317.

Don't let anyone convince you that a messy house is the sign of a messy mind. It's the sign of a woman who is out having a wonderful time.

318.

If you're too much of a
clean freak, people will start
to call you Howard Hughes
and you'll have to let
your toenails grow.

319.

Build a separate little hut
outside your house for your
husband's and sons' gym bags.

320.

Turn your kids loose with
Mr. Clean erasers and they'll erase
every spot and fingerprint in the
house and have fun doing it.